Jocelyn's Purpose

Rays of Hope After Stillbirth

Written by Andrea Waun

Foreword Written by Anthony W. Downen

PublishAmerica
Baltimore

ISBN: 1-60703-689-4
PUBLISHED BY PUBLISHAMERICA, LLLP
www.publishamerica.com
Baltimore

Printed in the United States of America

Foreword

It is somewhat of an awkward feeling to be writing the foreword to a book, written by someone so close to me to a tale of such pain. But it is in the end of all the things that come where we find true meanings, purposes, and understanding: not during the process of grief.

The person whose story you are about to read is of someone I have known, admired, and respected for nearly fourteen years. We were high school sweethearts for a time, but best friends for life. There have been many ups and downs to our friendship on both personal and spiritual levels that bond us together in an odd sort of fraternity of people who have lost a child due to stillbirth. From the get go, let it be known that you are not alone and simply because you don't hear advertisements or warnings for stillbirth while watching your TLC baby shows of what to expect, you are not alone and sadly not in a unique situation.

For my own part, there was a fear of losing the mother of my child due to some different complications. But losing my child didn't occur to me other than perhaps SIDS. There are a lot of anxieties that come with becoming pregnant for both women and men. The fear of being a good role model, being supportive, financial stability, moral instilled values, correct measures of discipline…etc. But unless you have had a previous complication during a pregnancy or miscarriage, or knew someone who had gone through what you now go through, it was more than likely a complete mystery.

What Andrea has done for you here in this short tale, is really give you a snapshot of a short period of her life: A period that will redefine her spiritually as well as personally. It all began of course with all the joys of the great news, beyond the gut wrenching words that delivered her the bad, and through the grief that floored her following.

If asked, she will not say that this story is about her being courageous, but once you have found your way through her explanations and anecdotal offerings to help you ease your transition from mother to be, you will see the courage it took to share this tale. It's not something everyone can do, and especially in this format for the world to view.

If you were looking at these first few pages for a table of contents to find your way through a 'how to cope with stillbirth', you will not find it listed here. Andrea's offering of support is that of someone giving you straight talk, a conversation of what she had to go through from top to bottom without so much as flinching for her personal privacy of such a delicate and personal matter.

It was very eerie to find the similarities in our situations with our separate stillbirth's, but comforting to know that I could help her. A comfort she is looking forward to pass on to you or the people in your life that have suffered this terrible, and regrettably far too common of a circumstance. As she will say throughout this book, everything happens for a reason, perhaps even you finding this book in your hands now. To pass on the experience and life of her little baby girl and find new life through a tale of hope, that you too will come to understand the purpose of your tragedy in the grand scheme of your life.

Jocelyn's Purpose

How do you sit down and write the story of your daughter's life two weeks after losing her? How do you write the story of your daughter's life when she never once saw the light of day? How do you write about those precious eight months when you felt her kicking, felt her hiccup, heard her little heartbeat, never knowing it would be all you'd ever have? The words are there and will come out, but with each word I write, my heart still continues to break.

For any mother who's been through this, knows the desperation of trying to get those most important memories on paper so as to never be forgotten—the story of her life that only I as her mother can tell. From beginning to end, a short story with so many dimensions that I won't be able to capture them all. However, from one grieving mother to another, I cannot rest until it's done. I cannot chance losing a special memory. Now what I write will not all be special or fond. Some will be just the plain truth which was part of her little life too.

And so I begin. With any story, the best place to start is at the beginning. So with that said, I begin the long and emotional story of my daughter Jocelyn's short but meaningful life. My husband Alex and I always considered ourselves spiritual people. We are both Catholic, and were both brought up by strong, loving families who not only had us in church every Sunday, but who also had us in extra church events. Since before we were married, we talked of having children one day and how we wanted them brought up in the Catholic Church as we were. Alex and I dated for six years before getting married on October 2, 2004. We loved each other very much on the inside, but on the outside, things could very often be a different story. Our lives were like roller coasters, up and down all the time. We'd have good days and bad days. We found ourselves heading down the wrong roads several times, becoming very selfish, but each time, one of us would bring the other out of it.

We were there for each other to say the least, but no matter how many scrapes or bad situations we got past, we still weren't proud of whom we were. We were becoming more and more negative until the day came when we didn't even like other people. We'd say rude comments to someone in passing if they even looked at us wrong. We continued to say we were spiritual people, but hardly ever went to church. Jobs were difficult, because we had gotten to the point where we couldn't tolerate other people, however both worked in settings where people were our number one business. Jobs came and went for me, but for Alex he kept his one. I could see that he was beginning to be kinder to others than I was, and started feeling pretty bad about myself.

The first part of our marriage changed a lot about who we were. Something about being married and not hiding the fact that we lived together was a burden off my shoulders. Not having to lie to my parents, who have always supported me, and simply marriage itself made us connect with reality again and see a little of the errors of our ways. We were happy anyway and that made us a little nicer to others. We began developing close friendships with good people and surrounding ourselves with family more. Even still, we were selfish. In June, we found out I was pregnant: A grand moment. I thought if anything can pull us together more than the marriage did, it's a baby. We were so excited. I called everyone I knew. From that point on, I was on cloud nine. Nothing could get me down. I didn't think there was anything in this world that could take away the happiness I felt.

For the next six weeks, life went on. I gloated and bragged constantly. During the six weeks I began bleeding. I figured it was nothing and I was just a little worried. Soon after came the contractions. The pain was intense. I ended up going to the hospital, which we were told that they wouldn't know anything until two days from then. Two days later, we found out that the baby we were so excited about was gone due to miscarriage. Life and everything around you suddenly stops at that time. Your heart along with the rest of your body goes numb and thoughts seem to be unable to stay long enough to understand.

You just sit there staring at the floor and say, "okay" to the doctor. A person who at that moment seems to own your world, able to nurture or shatter it with only words. I remember looking at Alex who in turn was looking at the floor. I could tell in his face that his heart had just been broken, and it broke mine to see his dream be washed away. To this day I can't say which one of our lives was shattered more that night. It is easy to say myself being the mother that carried the child. But a father has is own bond that can't be denied. It was our first child that we hoped for so long, but the concept of a miscarriage wasn't foreign to us. But even with that knowledge, you never think it will happen to you. Not in the middle of your life coming together and the wrongs you've made right making you feel that you have found the right path.

I decided from that point on, to be strong for him. You would just have to know the man. Such a big, strong, emotionally stable man that I had never seen cry. And now I see the soul within him needing comforting that I wasn't sure I could provide. But for him and all that he was to me, I had to be the rock and the shoulder for him to lean on as we moved through was seemed to be the biggest obstacle we would ever face. The whole way home that night we talked about God and his reasons. We spoke of our faith in him that he did this for a reason that we were sure was for our best interests. We called everyone and let them know of our loss and that we were hanging in. The lesson I learned from that baby at that time was about faith. Whoever that little form would of become had a purpose and that purpose I believe was fulfilled. As much as it hurt, I didn't know how weak my faith in the Lord had been previously. All I knew was that I needed it then. From then on, I just knew I would always have a strong faith to get me through what ever may come.

We held strong to each other and to our marriage. We decided that the best thing to do was to wait three months and then try again to have another baby. We did just that, and on February 22 of 2006 I found out I was once again pregnant. I didn't have a doctor, so from the insurance paperwork I picked a doctor based on name and the fact that it was a female. This to me would be my comfort for-a comfort I didn't even realize at the time would become so meaningful in my life.

On that day, my friend went to the clinic with me for my first visit. I remember my Doctor walking into the room for the first time. Physically looking at her, she was everything I'd wanted and more. I can't explain it. It's like you expect it to be someone else, but in reality, it felt like I'd known her for years. When I heard her voice, I knew I'd hit the jackpot. She was very professional, to the point, but sincere. She seemed to take a very special interest in our previous loss and sat down to talk with me longer on that visit than any doctor had ever talked to me. She had a name of course, but I refered to her as Doctor C. It didn't take long and I was hooked. I knew that I could put my trust in her and that everything would be okay, one way or the other. Her advice to me was as honest as it should be. "I don't know what will happen, but we've got to get you out of the first trimester." That is was stuck in my mind and was now my only goal. And with Dr. C in my corner I felt it only added to my faith and everything would be okay.

The first trimester, went quicker than I thought. I was still working, but couldn't physically or mentally do the work I needed to. I was becoming short tempered and agitated with the patients at the nursing home, and extremely worried about the lifting required. So I decided to quit and save myself those stresses. To me and Alex both this was what we needed. It was to be our first baby, and we wanted to make sure I didn't stress myself out. We knew in our hearts it was the best move. One salary was not easy, but proved to work in its own way. Alex in his kind, sincere, and modest way went to work diligently every day. He came home every night, happy to see me. These moments as I look back were some of our best.

At week 20, we went in for a sonogram and to find out what we were having. We were elated to find out we were having a girl. I was thrilled as I laid there on the table and I couldn't take my eyes off the screen. Alex and a friend who went with us, laughed when the baby kicked her little foot. I didn't see this, but was very happy Alex did. It's one of those moments that let's you know what a great father your husband is going to be. After the appointment I was on cloud nine. I had always wanted a girl, and my dream had come true.

I called everyone who would answer, and emailed the rest. I made sure to write "Great news! It's a girl. Jocelyn Nichole is due October 22. She currently weighs 13 ounces and is in great health." For the next five months or so, it was pregnancy bliss. Now if you ask my friends if bliss is the word they would use they would not agree, but on the inside I was dancing. I played music for her, read to her, sang to her, and of course ate all I could get my hands on. My favorites were cheese and milk; always dairy.

The months seemed to drag by slowly, but pretty soon, I had a big belly. Everyone said "she's going to be huge" "you won't make it till October" "she takes after Alex". I was happy she took after her daddy. I always wanted my baby born with dark hair and chubby little cheeks. As the months wore on, the nursery started coming together. Peek a Pooh was the theme. My parents moved back into town, and I helped them get their house ready. Ripped wallpaper down, helped pick carpet, paint appliances, and more. We started birthing classes when I was 32 weeks pregnant. That was when I really noticed how close

I was. Everyone in there was almost due, and I was right there with them.

During the last class, the fathers learned how to dress a baby. We as the mothers sat proudly admiring how great our husbands looked with that little plastic doll. I noticed that some of the dads were having too much fun with it, joking around. I also noticed one of the mother's moms who participated there with her daughter. She nudged her and pointed to Alex. I looked at Alex who was so diligently and ever so carefully trying to slip the baby's clothes over the hand so as not to touch the fingers. He was so into it, leaning real close and making sure it was all done perfectly. Anything the teacher said to do, Alex would slowly and carefully do. Another special moment that lets you know how great a father your husband will be. My heart was warmed, and I couldn't wait to see our own little bundle in his arms.

Such a big guy, but with such warmth and sincerity in his face and heart, that's my Alex. Soon after the classes started I began having contractions. The first time we didn't think they were real, but we went through the procedure anyway. We timed them, and noticed that they were coming about ten minutes apart. They weren't strong, but we figured what the heck, we'll make a practice run to the hospital. We packed up the car with our suitcases and clicked the car seat in. We were ready. The whole way, we laughed and joked around. It was a lot of fun.

We got there, and they hooked me up to monitors. I was having contractions, and they were coming three minutes apart. Since my Doctor was on call that weekend, I was put under the care of the one that was covering her. She at one point mentioned that if they couldn't stop the contractions, then they would talk about inducing and letting me deliver that day. However, they were able to stop the contractions, which meant simply that the labor was not real. I would later find out that real labor can only be slowed down but not stopped.

I went home the next day, but found myself back at the hospital with worse contractions. Better safe than sorry we thought. Once again they stopped the contractions and sent me home. My nerves were being shaken. I didn't know how I was supposed to tell when it was real or not. They felt pretty real to me at the time. A week passed, and I started feeling the heaviness of pregnancy. I felt completely weighed down, and started aching everywhere. I would still play music for her and read to her. One day I sat down and read the whole children's bible for her.

The day after that, Alex worked until ten at night. I had noticed that I hadn't felt her move in a long time. Since I had only woken up at two in the afternoon, I thought nothing much of it. Eight hours later when I still hadn't felt her move, I was more worried. I wondered if I should even tell Alex when he got home. We'd already been to the hospital twice, and both times been sent home. I figured I was just overreacting, but decided to tell him anyway. I honestly didn't think it was too big of a deal because she never moved much in that last month anyway. I told Alex, and although we were both worried, we decided it best to sit it out and see the doctor the next day.

That night I did every thing I could to convince myself and Alex that I had felt just the littlest move. I already had a sonogram scheduled the next day, so it was just convenient to wait. That was one of the longest nights of my life. The next day, we were running around on edge as we prepared to go to the doctor. Still not feeling her move, we headed out to the doctors office. When we turned from our street onto Blanco road, I looked into the sky and told Alex" isn't that the most beautiful sky you've ever seen?" It was kind of dark, but it had rays of sun shooting down from everywhere. Never in my life had I seen such a sky.

I was the first to bring it up to Alex instead of waiting for him to talk to me. I brought up the story of my friend Tony who lived in California. Tony and I were high school sweethearts that didn't work out after I graduated, but we always had a strong friendship. When he married his wife in 1999, they left for California. We went our separate ways, and lost contact for six years. During my fifth month of pregnancy, he found me online, and we began talking again. He had been through some rough times of his own and wanted to give me some insight. He mentioned that not only had he and his wife had a miscarriage, but they had also lost a full term baby at the very last minute. His son, Ian, was two days past due when they went in thinking she was in labor. They were horrified to find that there wasn't a heartbeat from the monitor and then had to get a sonogram done. He watched them do the sonogram and draw an arrow to an unmoving spot on the monitor and labeled it as the heart. It was several minutes before the doctor let his wife know that truth that he already knew; that they had lost their son.

The cord had become wrapped around their son's neck as he turned to come down the night before. He had passed away in the night and come morning her body had tried to deliver. It wasn't something they expected or even thought possible.

Nine months of hopes and dreams that vanished without warning or complications before hand.

Our hearts broke for them. I couldn't imagine the pain of losing a child so late in a pregnancy and the hell they must have gone through to get through that. I had only had a miscarriage and that hurt bad enough. Well, here we are on our way to our sonogram, so I felt one of us had to bring it up. "What if what happened to Tony happens to us" I asked very quietly to Alex not knowing how he would react. He let out a huge sigh and said "I was just trying to find the right words to ask you the same thing? We go on," he said. I said yeah, it's not like we haven't done this before, just not like this. He said I know. We talked about Tony and how we never really understood.

We then turned the topic to my brothers friends Ryan and Wendi who lost there son eight months after he was born. He never left the hospital. We talked about how these young couples made it through that kind of pain. We just couldn't understand it. "But if we do have to, we'll make it" I said. "If we go in there, and she's gone, we have faith, right?" That's all we can have he said. We walked in there, just after having the heaviest conversation of our lives, but still with so much hope that we were just scaring ourselves for no reason. We were called back and ventured into the room where our doctor met us.

The first thing I said was I haven't felt her move in a while. She was very nonchalant, and replied "well, she doesn't have a lot of room in there." I immediately let out a sigh and said yeah, that's what we thought too. It would be my last ray of hope. She placed the monitor to read the baby's heartbeat on my stomach and I held my breath. I heard gurgling noises, but no heartbeat. She began moving the monitor around slowly at first then a little faster. The whole time I stared at the monitor, desperately trying to see just one little movement.

I turned and looked at Alex and the look on his face was devastating. It was a look that for the rest of my life will haunt me. She looked at me and asked softly "when was the last time you felt her move?" As the first tear slid down my cheek I said about two days ago. She went and sat down on her stool, looking at her clipboard, and simply said "I'm sorry...I don't know what to say." I couldn't look at my husband, so just stared at the floor letting tears automatically run down my cheeks. She said she'd give us as long as we needed and after handing me a box of Kleenex she left the room. I began sobbing, and Alex came over and held me as tight as he could. Not even two minutes later, I pushed away from him and said lets go.

I walked out of the room and past the desk where Dr. C and some nurses were sitting. She told me to go to the hospital and that she would be there. We continued walking from the office next door to the hospital. Although the tears continued to fall, I was not crying. I knew I had to be strong for what I needed to do. I went to the phone in the hallway of the hospital. I could see the labor and delivery doors and knew they were waiting for me inside, but didn't care. There was one phone call I had to make and it would take every ounce of courage I had. I knew I would only have to say one line and then I could let it all out.

When my mom answered her phone with her normal chipper hello, my heart split into a million pieces and I couldn't talk. It took me a few seconds and another hello to barely get out the words. "We lost her." "What" was all I heard from the other end of the line. I repeated my self, voice cracking, and barely forcing the words out. "What happened?" she asked. Her voice was direct and took me off guard a little. I said, "I don't know."

I began sobbing quite uncontrollably at that time. She asked if Alex was with me and I said yes. She said they would be there as soon as they could and to stay in touch. Her voice had a very motherly and firm tone to it. I knew I didn't have to worry, they would be there. As I hung up the phone, I noticed just how heavy my chest felt. It felt like it would explode. I went in to the labor and delivery area for what I knew would be the last time. I knew this time, going into that room was—the time-. I knew as well that I wouldn't be carrying out a baby. They took me to a private suite by myself, and asked the basic admitting questions. I cried the whole time.

When Alex came back in, I just sat there staring at the ceiling crying. Nurses were hooking up IVs, the sonogram lady was hooking up her machine, and I felt like my world was collapsing on all sides. I didn't understand. It was all a huge puzzle and I sat there trying to piece it together, but none of the pieces made sense. How much am I supposed to try to figure out, and how much am I supposed to leave in God's hands here. Is there a lesson I'm supposed to learn here? It was all just a huge puzzle, and I was clueless to figure out what to do with it. I knew my daughter was safe and that comforted me. To know she would never be hurt—to know she would never have her heart broken—to know that I would never have to worry about her—me knowing that she was in Gods hands was the comforts I felt.

What broke my heart the most was my husband. I had

broken his heart, and I knew it. I had taken away the one thing that only a month ago he's told me was the best gift I could've given him for his birthday. To see the hurt on his face, the pain in his heart was maddening. Never in my life did I ever want to see those things on my husband. The most remarkable aspect of my husband is the way his eyes sparkle. That day, brimming with tears, was the most heart wrenching, painstaking thing to see. I felt like the sins I'd committed in my life had caused this. That my daughter was literally dying for my sins. And if this was true, unless I learned from her, could it be the difference of having children again or not? Could this be my test? I will never know if this is the test for future children, but I know I will "try like hell" as Alex has begun to say, to do the very best I can.

No, Alex was never perfect, but I have carried around the weight of my sins for a very long time, and I knew that weight would only be lifted if I suffered. I don't know how, but somehow I just knew that. I have pleaded for forgiveness from God for my sins for years and years, but the guilt I felt, never left. Sitting in that hospital room that day, and still today, I curse myself. It was me that was supposed to suffer, not my husband, who only wanted to be a good father. Not my parents who joyfully did all they could in anticipation for their first grandchild. Not his parents who for years have wanted the moment to see their grandchild and who for months shopped constantly for baby things. No, these were not the people who were supposed to suffer for my sins.

And my daughter, my little beautiful girl who will never get to grow up because of me would have to suffer for my sins. I knew sitting there that day looking at the ceiling that half of my suffering would come from those around me sitting and looking at me with broken hearts that at that time I felt I had broken. Now, these thoughts have pacified somewhat, but no one really knows how it happens or why. Maybe she did die for my sins as Jesus died for ours, or maybe it has nothing to do with that at all. I know that if she did die for my sins, and part of my punishment is to see the people I love most in my life suffer, then I must have done some pretty bad things, and I know I have.

When Alex sat down beside my bed, I felt comforted immediately. I remember, looking at him and telling him I was sorry. Tears continued to run down my cheeks. What happened next, broke my heart even more, but my husband, big guy, burst into tears and started apologizing to me for not cleaning up after himself at home and things like that. I immediately snapped into reality. Although, I could not look at him, I started talking to him clearly. I told him that it was going to be okay. That we still had each other and always would. That the Lord has her and will keep her safe, that we'll never have to worry about her. We talked a lot about her purpose. We didn't even have to think about it. Like our first child, who we immediately knew had a purpose to teach us about faith, our Jocelyn's purpose was to help her daddy and I to be better people. That was the bottom line of it.

Now we know she had many purposes on this earth, but her main purpose we were sure of was to make us better people. We swore that from that day on we would be different. In the name of our daughter we would be different. I told Alex "she can't die in vane. If this is part of why she died and we don't do anything to change who we are, then our little Joc," as I always called her, "would die in vane." No, I couldn't have that. I believe also that she was meant to bring us closer to God. I told Alex when our first baby died, we can get mad, we can blame whoever, but we must never blame God. I don't think we could've anyway, because our faith is strong. I just couldn't chance it. We had to know and believe one hundred percent that he took both of our children for a reason. That was one of the things that morning in the hospital room that pacified us the most. If one of us lost it, and even began crying, the other would simply have to say, she's safe—God has her.

We talked for much of the morning. Nurses came and went, offering apologies. Two yellow roses were placed on our door to let people know. It was a bittersweet morning. We managed to get all our crying out of the way, and start talking seriously about the few minor things we wanted. We even made the other person laugh once or twice. We decided that a funeral was what we wanted to her. I was very bold on that. I wanted her properly laid to rest. I also wanted her baptized. Those were the two most important things to me. Other than that everything seemed very empty. It all seemed so unreal. People would come to visit, and it would be like we were playing a game. As if we were talking about something that happened to someone else. Someone would say something that would make us laugh and we would feel guilty. There were so many emotions. It just didn't seem real.

We didn't know what to say to people. We hardly knew what to think. All I knew was that I had a baby in me, a baby that a few days ago would kick me and hiccup, and now there was no movement. All that remained was a big pregnant belly. I still found it hard to believe, though. It was like it was all so clear.

"Okay, we lost our baby, thanks, have a nice day," but on the flip side of the spectrum it was like, "is ths for real? Could there be some sort of mistake, both machines broken, she's just not moving, anything." At that point you start to grasp for something, anything, then before you get to it, you give up because you know in your mind that it's pointless. That's how this whole experience has been. Could it all be a dream? None of this makes any sense. It's all too clear one day, and really fuzzy on others.

We found out that day that my parents had hopped on a plane from Michigan, and were coming here. They would arrive that night, but wouldn't get to the hospital room until the morning. After a long day of visitors and a lot of medication, I passed out, awaiting the next day when I would give birth to a daughter that no longer lived. When I awoke the next day, I turned around to find my parents sitting in the room. It was so great to see them. They were my comfort now, and would be for a long time to come. I didn't know just how much they would help us out at that time, but I knew it was how great to see them.

I can't tell you a lot of what happened that day because I was drugged for most of it, but there were tears, and there were laughs. Overall, it was just good to have my parents there. They stayed with us almost the whole day, when I was asleep, awake, they were there. Dr. C broke my water around six that morning. For the rest of the day, anything I wanted I got. The nurses catered to me like I was a queen. They were so very nice. At around one in the afternoon, I started having some pretty heavy contractions—okay, they were very heavy. At that time I opted to do the epidural, and despite what all the others have told me about not even feeling it, you do feel it. Just being honest. After the epidural set in, I think the line went something like this. "I am at peace with myself and with others." I was drugged up with more than the epidural, and very happy for it. I believe I even talked to my brother on the phone. What was said I can't remember, but I know he said later that I was gone.

At around five o clock p.m. or a little after, I began pushing. A process my doctor would later say was an absolute disaster, because the shoulders got stuck. At five-thirty eight, my little baby girl was born. Dark hair, chubby cheeks. Nothing can capture the moment of when they place your child on your chest and they feel so warm and soft. No one can capture the moment when they place your lifeless baby on your chest. The tears immediately come, and you feel so helpless to help her. Yet, she was so warm, and so soft, and I could imagine that she was just sleeping. Oh, how beautiful she was. No words. My sweet little baby girl laying in a blanket, snuggled under my chin. There were just simply no words. When the nurse took her from me to have her cleaned up, I burst into tears. My parent came to my side in an instant. I just kept crying. I felt so helpless. I was so hurt, and so very sorry. Sorry for everything.

I immediately began blaming myself despite what anyone said. It didn't matter now, I'd been blaming myself for days, so what did it matter now. I'd seen her lifeless form, and knew exactly who at that moment to blame. For most of my life I have had very low self esteem. I don't know why, but I did. I never thought anything I did was good enough. I felt like I was just lazy and helpless. I never finished tasks, or could ever hold a job for long. Now, faced with this, it seemed like just another task I couldn't finish. I knew I had to stop, and to put my faith in God. I knew I couldn't blame myself. It was just so hard. After all, it had already happened twice. I guess sometimes we just aren't supposed to know all the answers. I did know one thing, though. This experience would be one of my greatest tests of strength.

Finally the time came to hold her again. I had been so anxious the whole time she had been away, because I didn't know where she was. You can emotionally lose her one day, but to physically lose her the next put me in complete distress. I didn't know what to do with her when they brought her back, but I still wanted her. This was an anxiety I'd learn to get to know well in the next few days. When they gave her to me again, my parents got to see her for the first time. They asked if I wanted them to leave so we could spend time with her alone. I said no. All I wanted was for them and Alex's mom to gaze upon her; my beautiful daughter. I didn't know how much time we'd have with her. I didn't know if once I gave her back I'd ever see her again. I didn't know anything.

I did however know I wanted my parents to capture as much of it as possible. I held her for a good while and we had our first mother and daughter picture taken together along with our first family photo. Alex opted not to hold her which at the time I couldn't blame him because everything was new to us. No one knew what to do or think. At least we didn't. Yes, I wanted him to hold her very badly, but I also wanted to hear my daughter cry and see what color her eyes were, so point rested. I asked my parents if they wanted to hold her, and more proudly than ever, placed my pride and joy into the arms of my father. He carried her over to the couch, and he and my mom sat with her. The second time in my whole life I'd seen my dad cry, and he had my daughter in his arms. I had to look away.

My mom held her next, and was everything I pictured she would be—a proud grandma. Alex's mom opted not to hold her as well, but was there for her baby which was okay with me. They handed her back to me and I couldn't keep my eyes off her. The thing I remember most was how her lip looked so pouty. We laughed and said she definitely took after me on that one. My dad came over and took off one of her little pink lacy socks (her right foot), and we looked at that tiny little foot that just days ago hadn't seemed so small. He gently put her little sock back on. The chaplain came in and everyone stood around the bed as she placed a bib on my daughter that had a cross on it and said "child of God" on it. She said some passages and then from a tiny little seashell she dripped water on my daughters head. My daughter was baptized, if only it was the action of doing it, it was done.

I knew where my daughter's soul was, so this was mainly done to pacify myself. We all just sat there for a long time as I held her. In my head I was telling her how sorry I was, and how much I loved her. I just kept repeating those things in my head. "Mammas so sorry baby, I'm so so sorry this happened…momma loves you so much, I'm so sorry" My parents had decided to leave the room, and I could feel my whole body shutting down. My mind was very rapidly closing off. I could feel it, and I knew I was done. Alex's mom and sister were still in the room along with the chaplain, and I was beyond done with people. I was done, I can't explain it. I pushed the button frantically still with my daughter Jocelyn in my arms and asked that a nurse come and get her.

I got very frustrated when they didn't understand me and I had to repeat it. "I need someone to come take the baby." I couldn't even associate her as mine at that time, I just said "the baby". When she came and took her I kissed her on the head not knowing if I'd ever see her again and thinking I'd said everything I needed to. Thinking I could and would be fulfilled by that few moments with her I'd just had. I just laid my head back and felt the emptiest I'd ever felt in my life. I couldn't believe I'd sent her back, but also knew I couldn't bare to hold her either. I just laid there. I don't want to say I didn't care, because I did, almost too much, but I just felt so empty.

We went about the night. My parents brought me food, but I just couldn't eat for anything. Later, the nurse came back and asked me point blank "do you want to hold Jocelyn again?" This wasn't in my plan, and had never been. I had figured it was done, that I was done, and that this empty feeling I was feeling was what I would live with forever. That the kiss I'd placed so lovingly on her forehead would be the last, there really was never to be another chance to hold her. I was confused and without thinking gave a firm "no". A no that even jolted the nurse a bit because she asked "you don't?" After that, she brought in my memory box and placed it on the table below my bed, right in my line of vision.

The tears had already become sobs even twenty minutes before, so I was crying pretty hard. Poor Alex just didn't know what to do. I just sat there crying as hard as I could not having a care as to who walked in, not caring who heard, or even if I woke up the person in the next room. I just cried and cried with my husband ever so loyal sitting by my side holding my hand. I cried for my daughter, my little girl, my new angel. I cried for the things I'd done for the way I made everyone feel, for my selfishness over the years, for my petty immaturity. I cried for my Grandma, who had passed away the week before, and who I'd meant to see, but didn't. But mostly I cried for my baby. I wanted to hold her so bad, to take her home, to change her diaper, to rock and sing to her just one more time. To hear her call me mamma, to see her in my husbands arms, I simply just cried-I cried for my Jocelyn.

The next day I was told I could leave whenever I was ready. I was ready, but still felt a huge connection to the room where I'd been pregnant, gave birth, seen and held my daughter for the first time. The tears had diminished and I was really starting to feel like I could get through this okay. A mind trick that would play me for a fool a lot in the next few weeks. Because in reality it was not okay, and the next few days, unbeknownst to me would be the hardest, yet best days of my life.

We decided the best thing for everyone would be to stay at my parent's house as much as we could. We knew nothing as a young couple of what to do, what needed to be done, or even how to think straight. So we opted that the best thing now would be not to add another obstacle of going home and sitting doing nothing to ourselves. This proved to be a wise choice. My parents immediately set into motion, handling all calls and arrangements that needed to be made. There were choices that needed to be made, and either we could do them as her parents, or my parents would. We both decided in the name of our daughter, and as to not regret anything later, to be as much a part of the planning as we could, no matter how heart wrenching it would be. I also decided in my head somewhere that I had to hold her again. I needed more time, and it had to be done. I became very adamant about that. I didn't care about anything else. I had to hold my baby girl again.

I had to give myself and her every opportunity to be together. I could think of nothing else than that I had to hold my baby. This feeling, plagued with anxiety would haunt me for the next few days. I would not rest until that horrible, wicked, ugly feeling of guilt and loneliness left me. Until I knew that I had done everything in my power to take care of my child while she was with me. To make sure she had everything she needed. This was my time to be her mother, and I wasn't going to fail. I would not let her down. You know that old saying there's always tomorrow? Well, in this case, there really wasn't. I had to get as much done as I could. It was all for me. It was to pacify myself, because this wasn't my daughter, and I knew it.

My daughter was in heaven, dancing around in the clouds, her soul resting in the hands of our Lord. I knew this, but physically, I still had to be her mamma. I couldn't and wouldn't let her down, and I knew at some point I would have to forgive myself for the sins of my past, that I did not need something else in my life to blame myself for. I was adamant. Nothing would take these moments from me. For in my mind I had already robbed myself of holding her the night before.

That first night after we were released from the hospital, we decided it would be best to spend the night at our own apartment. I knew my parents had gone in and changed her room, and I very nervous to see what it would look like. When we opened the door to our apartment, we noticed that little was changed. I noticed a new rug in the kitchen, and the little shelf that used to be in my daughters room, now sat on a small wall as you first walk in. I could tell from where I stood at the front door looking down the hall that the door to her bedroom was closed. I walked straight to it, and put my hand on the knob.

As I began to turn it, Alex came from behind and said, "no, don't do it, not yet." I said, "we have to, it's the only way". Something inside me was searching for an end point, a closure to this nightmare that didn't seem to end. I opened the door, and we both walked in. Where her crib had once sat now laid a double sized bed. On the wall where we were temporarily keeping her stroller, sat a long dresser, and in the same spot that only a few days prior I had sat on the floor and read the entire children's bible to my daughter sat a taller dresser. Curtains had been placed on the window above where her little shelf of books had once been. It all looked so different, so beautiful. I loved it for a spare bedroom, but in the same way, was able to trick my mind into seeing what use to be there. I cried until Alex made me leave the room. The door was shut, and wouldn't be opened until I could get past this.

I remember going to the funeral home to pick out her grave. I knew I wanted her buried under a tree. I also knew what kind of coffin I wanted for her. I knew I would be picking these things, and I didn't care. The first question from my mouth to the man was can I hold my baby again? When? He said she was not there yet, but I could make an appointment for the next day and hold her for as long as I could. My heart was put at ease, and at the same time I was immediately filled with an overpowering anxiety. Could I wait that long? How long should I hold her for? I want to hold her as long a I can" One day's not enough" How do I put her down after and leave her?

Should I be doing this", "There's so much I have to say to her" I love you, I'm sorry, You're my angel now, I need to write these down? My mind was ready to explode.

We went and picked her coffin and her place of rest, which also pacified me and filled me with anxiety again. Yes, it's weird, but the two of those can occur at the same time. I thought is this place going to be good enough for her? How much is that coffin? Oh Lord how are we going to pay for this? What do I put in there with her: Her blanket, yes, her blanket, and a rosary. She must have a rosary. What else? I don't want to forget a thing. Are you supposed to put stuff in there? I know her soul leaves with nothing, but oh to leave her in there by herself.

Back to holding her, oh I can't wait, I need to know where she is. Has the autopsy happened yet? Oh how long should I hold her? PICTURES I have to have pictures. As soon as I get back to mom and dads I have to put the camera in my purse. I can't forget the camera. Where is the camera? The thoughts whirled through my head like a hurricane, hence the reason for the anxiety pills prescribed by Dr. C. I had wondered what they were for, and now I knew.

The next day was to me—the day-. Absolutely one of the best days of my life. I was overly excited about seeing my daughter. It seemed like forever since I'd seen her, and I just had to get to her side. I suppose it had a lot to do with carrying her so close for so long and then being separated. Either way, I knew I hadn't slept the night before, and wouldn't calm down until I saw her. My chest felt tight, and I was having the most anxiety I'd felt all day long. When the time finally came, we all got in the car and headed to the funeral home. I was nearly hysterical because we were supposed to be there at five o'clock and were running a few minutes behind. When we arrived after a car trip that seemed like we'd driven a hundred miles instead of five, we were told to wait in the sitting room.

My mind was racing, my heart beating a mile a minute. I didn't know what to expect. They had told me she would be laid on a table when I got in there with just a onesie on. I would later be able to dress her in what we called her "princess gown". A gown Alex's mom picked up for her. She also had a little pink headband with lace and flowers, and tiny pink shoes. I was excited to dress her for the first and only time, but at that time just wanted to see her. When the man came out and asked if I was ready to see her, I nearly flew out of my seat. The plan was that I would go in for fifteen minutes by myself, and that Alex would come in with me after that. When I entered the room, I could see her laying there on the table.

My heart immediately melted. There she was. Every step I took toward her, I noticed just how much more beautiful she got. She was an angel. Never in my whole life had I seen a prettier little girl. They had wrapped plastic around her arms and legs and had a piece coming out from behind her head. "It almost looks like a halo" the man said. I hadn't even realized that he had remained in the room with me. I didn't care either. We were together, and nothing was going to take me from her now. I took a few pictures of her, and told her how beautiful she was. I told her how much I loved her, and placed my hand where I *knew* she had an incision from the autopsy, and told her how sorry I was for that. I cried and just continued to say I love you baby, Mamma loves you so much. I was aching to just grab her and hold on to her as tight as I could, but as I thought of picking her up, I realized I was very nervous, and wasn't even sure how to do it.

I knew her skin was fragile and the last thing I wanted was to hurt it, so I turned to the man behind me. "How do I pick her up?" I asked. Mother or not, there are some things you just don't know I suppose. "Can I just pick her up?" "Absolutely", he said. Something about this man always put me at ease. Such a nice young man with nice soft features and a very soft voice. "Okay?" I said as a question more than a direct answer. As I picked my daughter up for the first time, and carried her to a chair, I noticed how heavy she was. Such a big girl. Just like her daddy. Then I realized it. It couldn't be this way. Something was missing. As much as I was in heavenly bliss with her in my arms, something was definitely missing. I turned to the man, with tears in my eyes, hoping I wasn't making another big mistake by not spending more time with her alone, and said "can you bring in my husband please".

No, the fifteen minutes were definitely not over but as soon as he came over and stood by my side, it was all right. Our family was together, and I felt my body just relax. Without thinking, I blurted the next words out, not even knowing where they were coming from. I looked up at Alex who was standing at my left side and with a slight bit of desperation in my voice softly asked "do you want to hold her". I couldn't believe I had asked knowing how he felt, knowing he just didn't feel right about it. His answer took me aback a bit when he said "do you want me to". Just as simple as that—"do you want me to?" Kind of like he thought I was just waiting for him to ask? "I really do", I told him. He sat down and the moment I'd waited for since the day I knew we wanted children together was here. I placed my precious daughter into the arms of her daddy. My heart simply melted.

I knew it wouldn't be long before he would ask me to take her back, so I could do one of two things. I could stand there and admire the moment and keep it in my heart forever, knowing this is all I'd ever have, or I could run like hell and just start clicking as many pictures as I could knowing that he probably didn't want any. It was a very selfish, but beautiful moment. Alex had his daughter in his arms and I could've cared less if I had his consent or not. I remember, circling around him clicking pictures as I went. One more I'd say, okay just one more, that's a good one, one more. The man standing by the door must of thought of me as a lunatic or something. Once again, these were my only moments, and I was capturing what I could.

The man asked if we wanted a picture taken of our family with Alex holding her. Hell yeah! Okay, I don't think I said that, but I definitely thought it. When Alex asked me to take her back, I did, and was at peace. For me, my heart was soaring on cloud nine. Jocelyn had been safe and secure in both of her parents arms just once, but she had. She had felt the warmth of our arms around her tiny body. She had been in her daddy's arms, and to me that was the single most wonderful, heartfelt moment of my entire life. She was held, and even though she wasn't living, she was still held in our arms.

We asked the rest of the family to come in shortly after, and for the next two hours I held my daughter. I dressed her in her princess gown; long, white and full of sparkles. I put one of her little pink shoes on (her right one). It fit perfectly, just like Cinderella. She looked perfect; my little angel. She was absolutely perfect. I rocked her and we listened to music together. I kissed her and we had lots of pictures taken in her dress. My brother and his wife, also Jocelyn's Godparents came in a little later and got to see their niece for the first time. They held her and exclaimed how pretty she was and how much she looked like Alex. Finally the time came when they were ready to start her viewing.

This had been a last minute decision the day before when we went to pick out her casket. We hadn't planned on having one, but I wanted everyone to see how beautiful my baby girl was. Since I was still holding her, they asked everyone to wait outside for a few minutes. I knew what I had to do. I knew I had to place my daughter inside her casket. I walked over and laid her gently inside. What happened next I can't explain, but I burst into tears, and balled. I cried and cried. The only explanation I have was that it was the first time I had ever actually associated my daughter as not living. Yes, I knew it, but your head and your heart can say very different things. As friends and people from our church poured in, I balled.

We were having a viewing—a viewing for my daughter. It was all beginning to hit me way too fast. My head began spinning fast. Only moments ago she had just been sleeping, sleeping peacefully. But she's in a casket, and there was people, so many people that I was panicking. I could barely stand on my own two feet. I would collapse for sure, I knew it. Everyone was hugging me and I wanted to hit someone. Nothing seemed to have an order to it inside me. My nerves, heart, and mind all stretching past their limits while unable to control a bit of it. It was all so calm and peaceful only moments ago. I was swaying back and forth with my daughter in my arm, swaying to the music. The family was there and everything was perfect. What was going on? I was lost.

I had to get up to the casket. I had to be near my daughter. I thought about running up, grabbing her out of there and running away with her. I wanted to get as far from there as I could; somewhere, anywhere. A place where she would always be asleep and I could hold her for the rest of my life. I just stood there, frozen in place. When most of the people had left, Alex turned to me and said "what was that all about." He had seen me sobbing uncontrollably the whole time, but he didn't understand. How could he? No one knew my pain. All I wanted was to hold her, or even to touch her. To go stand with her as people passed staring down at her. To hold her little hand and say, "don't worry my little angel, pretty soon this will all be over and mamma will have you in my arms again."

'Hurry up' is all I kept thinking as people kept coming in and just standing around mingling. 'Screw it', I thought, and several times left my chair to go hold her hand or plant a kiss on her forehead. Alex kept coming and pulling me away from her. I was mad. No one understood. Not him, not anyone here. This is all the time I have. She's three feet from me and I can't go see her?

I stared helplessly at my child. I felt completely and utterly helpless. There she lay, within arms reach, and I was in hell trying to figure out a way to be with her. I don't have tomorrow to spend all day with my child like everyone else in this room. Three feet away and I couldn't get to her, couldn't hold her, couldn't touch her. At one point I stood up and walked over to her. Alex said something to try to stop me. I didn't care. I took the necklace from around my neck that had "Jocelyn" on a grain of rice on the inside of it, and placed it in her hand. If I couldn't be with her, I would at least get something accomplished while all these people stood around gossiping about things that could be gossiped about another day, or while Alex sat beside me cracking jokes.

My world was spinning. I knew I would get to hold her after this thing was over for a little while, and I knew that the next day before the funeral I would be able to again for a short while, but everything was spinning. I didn't know how long I'd have with her after this. I kept looking over to see who was still in the room. "Leave", I thought to my self. "hurry up and leave".

Before too long, I began to relax more, and soon after everyone except close family had left. I bounced up to where she was and got her out of there. I held her with so many things rushing through my head. Will they take her away again? At some point I will have to put her back in there again. How long do I have with her? I love you baby, mamma loves you so much. I held her and talked to her for a while, but still thoughts of having to leave her overtook me. I can't do this anymore, I thought to myself, panic once again setting in. I just can't do this. Mamma loves you baby I said to her. I stood up quickly, put her in her casket, kissed her on her forehead, and sped out of the room.

I was blinded by something stronger than myself. My chest was so tight, and I couldn't breath. When I got into the foyer, I burst into tears, and just cried. I knew my time that day was up with her. My precious daughter would be alone tonight, and I couldn't stay with her. If only they'd let me stay with her from this minute till the last minute. It was all the give her back, here she is, give her backs that were slowly eating me up on the inside. The funeral home director walked up to me and put her arms around me: A nice lady. The man was still my favorite, but a nice lady. She said the words that at the time I needed to hear. I will be here tonight. I will take care of her and watch out for her for you, okay? I nodded, and felt my chest loosen up a bit more.

Thinking about it now, I don't even think funeral homes are open at night, but it worked for me then, and gave me what I needed to leave her. My sister in law, Casey, put her arm around me and said "come on" you've been through enough today. We'll take you home. I felt bad about leaving Alex, but just couldn't stay there. After I got into their truck, I was fine again. All the way back to my parent's house, she told me how strong I was, and that if this was her, she wouldn't be able to be as strong as me. She told me she'd always known me to be one of the strongest people she knew. Words I didn't mind hearing after exerting more courage in one day than I'd felt I'd given in all my life.

When I got to my parents house, I went to lie down on the couch and fell immediately asleep until Alex called to see if I was all right. He and my parents came home about an hour after we'd gotten there. Alex's Dad had gone to the funeral home, and I would later find out had said the whole rosary for my little girl. Alex and I went home, preparing ourselves for the next day when we knew we would have to say good-bye for the final time.

The next day was the day I'd dreaded the most since I first found out what day it was. It was Tuesday morning, the day of our daughter's funeral. The horrible day we would lay her to rest. Before that, though I knew I still needed to hold her for the final time. I was scared to death of what it would be like to have to put her down for the last time and turn and walk away. My heart was being pulled in all directions. I wanted to throw up.

When we arrived at the funeral home, we were a little early, and wondered if we should go in. I said yes, if it's unlocked, I'm going in. When we opened the door, there ahead of us stood the staff of the funeral home; all lined up with their arms folded in front of them. A beautiful tribute to our family and what they knew would be so very difficult for me to do. My whole life lay in the next room and I would only have a short time until I would have to say good-bye to that forever. It was torture, complete and utter torture. I didn't have to do this to myself, I knew. Several times, I almost said to my parents, tell them to get her ready, I can't see her again. I knew though that if I went this route, the tugging at my heartstrings I was feeling at this time would never go away. I would feel that huge weight on my heart for the rest of my life. I couldn't do that.

No, I would go in there, hold her, say my last words, and just keep her in my arms for as long as I could. We had planned in order to make it easier on myself, that I would hand her over to my parents and that they would place her into her casket for the final time. I just couldn't bare to hand her over to a stranger. I told my mom to give me fifteen minutes. I told her "I have to have a time limit or I'll go crazy" Alex and I went in there, and I walked toward my child with tears already in my eyes. I picked her up and walked to the chair where I sat down with her. I held her for several minutes. I rocked her to the lullaby that repeatedly played from the cassette in the corner.

This was to be our last time to be together. Back and forth I swayed with such a heavy heart. "Mamma loves you baby. You're my angel", I told her.

My mom came into the room. I asked her if she wanted to hold her again. She said no, that's okay, but after a minute said yes, actually I do. I handed her to my mom, glad to have another chance afterwards to hold her again. It was like I got to hold her twice that morning instead of just once. My mom started swaying with her back and forth in her arms. She looked at me and smiled. "I couldn't ever understand why every time you held her you swayed with her." She said. "There's something about having a baby in your arms that makes you sway." I said yeah.

As she handed her back to me, I knew it would be the last time I would receive her. My mom left the room and with my daughter in my arms and my husband by my side, we said our last good-byes to the sweetest of angels who had changed our lives forever. "We love you so much", I told her. "You need to be our liitle angel now. You need to give mommy and daddy strength now. It's going to hurt really bad. Mommy and daddy are going to hurt real bad because we are going to miss you so much, but we'll go visit you, and we'll be okay. Don't worry yourself over us, baby. We'll always think of you and talk about you. We're so proud of you. You're so beautiful. Daddy and I know where to find you, so you just wait there for us, we'll find you. You be our angel, okay."

I told Alex I was ready, and to tell my parents. He said "do you want me to take her?" I was floored. "Okay", I said, and placed my daughter lovingly into his arms. We both walked toward the casket, Alex with his daughter in his arms. He placed her in her casket and we fixed her dress to make it straight and made her look real pretty. I then kissed each of her hands, and kissed her forehead. Alex placed his hand on her head. We stood above her, looking proudly down at our sleeping daughter—a family of three standing together for the last time. We told her we loved her so much and to be our angel. We then, turned and left the room without a tear in our eyes. Our daughter and the good Lord above had given us the strength we'd needed to walk away that last time.

The funeral itself was not as hard as I had originally thought it would be. We rode over with Michael and Casey, and stood outside the mausoleum where I knew my child was finally resting and her casket closed. I felt a peace knowing that she was there, knowing I didn't have to worry anymore. Our last good-byes had been said and that had given me more closure than I had thought it would. I walked into the church, and Alex and I sat in the front pew of the small little chapel with Michael and Casey at our side and mine and his parents behind us. There is nothing in this world that can capture the feelings of two parents standing four feet away from the casket of their infant daughter—nothing. It was a jolt to see the casket closed. I knew she was inside, but almost had to keep reminding myself that she was. I began panicking again. My heart racing, I thought to myself "What if she's not in there? Which direction is she lying in? What if the cross we had placed in the casket with her fell and hit her head? Did they take the plastic off of her arms and legs? I hope we have everything in there. We did leave Alex's rosary in there didn't we?"

I stopped myself and made myself think of something else. "She is at peace now. She's fine." But oh, how I wanted to run up there and get her out and hold her just one more time. "NO, it's done," I had to keep reminding myself. Before long, the mass was started. Msgr. Fater who is a close family friend and also the priest who presided over Alex and my wedding said some beautiful words. I sniffled through the whole thing, but was doing better than I thought I would. They said some little prayers for Jocelyn, and sprinkled water on her casket. This was where I started breaking down.

Standing over my daughter's casket was a wonderful family friend. I was touched by his words, and was very happy those little prayers had been said by him. The time finally came when the song On Eagles Wings started playing. A very difficult song to get through at anyone's funeral let alone your daughter's. However, it was a very meaningful and inspirational song. A song I was proud to have sung at my child's funeral. "And He will raise you up on eagle's wings—bear you on the breath of dawn—make you to shine like the sun—and hold you in the palm of His hand"

During the beginning of the fourth verse, Alex and my brother left the pew and took hold of the two sides of the casket. It was an honor to see my husband carrying our daughter to her resting place. The last thing you ever want in life is to see your husband on the side of your child's casket, but when you've been through all we had at that time it was a wonderful tribute to her. When I got in line behind them and paraded out behind my daughter, I burst into tears and sobbed the entire way out.

My parents were again at my side. It was a beautiful moment, my daughter being laid to rest under the tree in Baby Land with all the other infants, but oh how my heart was breaking. My mom whispered into my ear as we were walking out of the chapel. "She's fine, her Daddy has her." I nodded between sobs. We made it to the tree, and I sat in the front row. It was beautiful. Her casket, just amazingly gorgeous with her flowers an top and her ribbon reading Jocelyn Nichole draping down. I looked to my left and saw the man from the funeral home standing with his arms crossed in front of him. The man I barely knew with those ever so soft facial features that always put me at ease. Once again he did just that. I knew he wouldn't leave until my daughter was properly laid to rest and that he had and would continue to do his job to the best of his ability. He was who I needed to see at that time I guess.

More words were said, but I just couldn't hear them. In only a few moments, I would have to walk away. I would have to leave her. I wanted to ask to see her just one more time after everyone left. Just open it a little and let me peek in. Let me hold her hand one more time. I knew it was highly inappropriate, but that my daughter would not be able to properly rest until she knew I was at peace. I had to do it for her. When everything had been said and people started walking to their cars my mom said, "You can stay with her for a little while if you want." "I can't I just don't want to ever leave her." I began to cry again as Alex's dad came to my side and put his arm around me. "She's our little angel now," he said with all the pride of a grandfather could muster. I nodded. He repeated, "She's our little angel."

I knew I had to just walk away, and so I did. I left my little girl in the hands of the man with the nice facial features. The comforting stranger who reminded me a lot of my husband and some how brought me to an ease. Yes, I knew could do that. After all, she was in Baby Land. She wasn't by herself—in fact, she had many, many new friends. When we got to the truck, my mom said "did you hear the tractor start up." I said no. She said a tractor had started up right as father had finished speaking. She said it was like it was Grandpa and Grandma saying 'don't worry, we've got her.'

My mom's voice broke in the middle, and my heart broke for her. Just twelve days before my daughter passed, my mom's mother had. Her dad was already in heaven. My grandpa was a farmer, hence the story of the tractor starting up. I knew she was safe too. She was in heaven, dancing in the clouds. My beautiful girl was up there in the sky, dancing in the clouds. She was laid to rest, and although my heart continued to break for my daughter I'd never get to know, I had closure.

The next few days were a blur. We stayed mostly at my parents, but spent the nights at our own apartment. I talked to my good friend Tony in California daily. Having previously been through this before with his son Ian, he walked us through it. He wrote us long detailed letters, comforting us, and letting us know that what we were feeling was normal, continuously adding in stories from his experience. I was happy to have this. I needed this, and if there was a day that I didn't hear from him I would be frantic.

He was one of our angels during this time. I continued to grieve for my daughter for the next week. It was strong and overpowering. I felt so heavy, so empty, and so alone. I clung to my husband with a new fear of losing him too. I don't know where it came from, but it would continuously haunt me. Still, the letters from Tony would come, and comfort us. It was basically the same stuff everyone else had been trying to tell us, but only Tony had been through this. He knew when no one else did.

Something special I don't think he'd mine me sharing is how he found his closure. He and his wife didn't have plans to remain in California and so didn't want to bury him there. They had him cremated to be taken with them where ever they moved to. But to have a special place to go to, they went to the first place they planned on going with their baby boy. The day after his wife was released from the hospital, they went to the beach in Oceanside and walked the shoreline until they found a perfect sea shell. Tony had already gotten both of them charms of sea shells for their necklaces and had a sea shell burned into Ian's Urn.

They dug a little hole and placed the shell in it. Together they said all the things I said and their own wishes, prayers, and sorrows. Together they buried it and took note of where they were. 753 is what they came up with. Seventh pillar out on the pier and they counted their steps to the pier noting fifty-three steps. It was their road map to their special, unmarked place of mourning. The idea was that during low tide he would be playing on the beach, and later in the day splashing about in the water. And no matter where they moved, all oceans lead to all rivers and they could go to any beach or river in the world and be with him.

At that time hearing this story, I felt an overwhelming connection to what this, my friend was telling me. I felt as though our lives were intertwined somehow. When he told me about the number 753 I immediately wrote back and told him of our number. Two. We found out we were pregnant on February 22 and were given a due date of October 22. Jocelyn was born on September 22 in room 2. It wasn't as sentimental as their 753, but to me, it meant something. And to add another seemingly supernatural twist, 7-5= 2 and 5-3= 2. It was just another coincidence that seemed to tie our tragic ordeals together and bring us closer as friends. It may not mean anything, but somehow it helped.

I believe that no matter how simple these coincidences were, they were enough to make me fully realize at that time that other people did go through this type of thing. They made me believe that these petty little things I was coming up with in my head about the numbers when I was supposed to be thinking about my daughter really might mean something. Maybe it was just to get me on the same page as what Tony was trying to tell me. It's at these times that you hear but don't understand. Everything Tony said to me, I heard and understood. It seemed to be the only voice I could hear. We would find out later that more coincidences lied in the wake of our losses.

On October 2, we went out to the cemetery to visit Joc for the first time. It was our two year wedding anniversary, and that was where we wanted to be. We stopped by the office first to pick out her headstone. I was so excited to get it so I could go and tell my daughter that it was on its way. We sat down, chose and a mahogany headstone. We had originally chosen black, but at the last minute decided black would be elegant and would make the grey lettering stand out more, but would not be good enough for our Joc. We had a cross engraved on the side that said Safe with Jesus on it. On the top we wrote 'Forever Our Angel', then her name and birthday underneath. It would be beautiful. We then picked out her little flower holder that would be placed in the ground in front of her headstone. The man told us we could pick out any one we wanted, and he would place it out there for us at no charge. He was another very nice man.

It is kind of odd but reassuring that the people who work in the business of other people's pain and mourning somehow seem to be chosen specifically for you. That everything seems to be exactly to your liking even without specifying a thing. The temperature at the funeral home is perfect, flower arrangements, attitudes, just enough of a smile to show kindness but not to be bubbly in your dark hours. These aren't things that are asked of you, yet they never seem to be an issue at any funeral I've attended.

We then headed toward that spot under the tree. "Baby Land" I was there. Finally, I was there. "Hi baby" I said "Mamma's here" I sat down on the ground beside her and put my hand on the freshly churned dirt that lay atop where she now laid. "We got your headstone today baby, so now you'll have one too," I told her. I stood up and Alex and I said a prayer for her. Alex then read her the poem I'd written for her while I was pregnant with her. A poem she was buried with. We then said the Our Father. I sat back down beside her. It seemed kind of empty. It was different needless to say.

When I could literally hold he those final two days, I could talk and say anything that went through my head. Now, as I sat here with my hand sifting dirt through my fingers, I felt lost to find the words to say to her. It had been a lot easier to talk to her when she was in my arms, however, on the reverse side, while I held her, I was having a lot of anxiety. Everything had to get out that needed to be said, but sitting here knowing she was resting peacefully, there was no anxiety. I figured everything had been said that needed to be said. Now, we just let her know we're here and let her continue resting.

I sat for a while, until Alex mentioned to me something about a grave beside her. I got up and walked over to where he was standing over a grave right next to Jocelyn's. Where did that come from I said? I don't know he replied. It's not a boy is it? I asked "Yeah", he said. WHAT? The story on that is that when we originally went out to pick out her place of rest, I had made a joke saying I didn't want her buried around any boys. We purposely put her around three little girls. Neither of us had seen this one and it lay right beside hers. "It's been here since July," Alex said I wonder why we never saw it before I said. I asked what the baby's name was. Maybe I had seen it, but I doubted it since the joke had been made—no boys. Alex bent down, then looked up at me. What is it I asked again. Ian—he said. You're joking, right! Please tell me you're joking. Ian was the name of the son my friend Tony had lost do to stillbirth only two years prior. I couldn't believe it. Do you want to know the first name, Alex said, starting to have fun with me since he knew he was shocking me to the core. What ? I asked. Gabriel, he said. This is the name of Tony's other son that they had a year after Ian passed. Please tell me you're kidding, I said. There's no way. It's not possible. I looked into the sky, and I was immediately filled with peace. "You found him, Joc, you found Ian." I was crying already. It was literally amazing. The angel who had so patiently sat there for the past week and a half, talking to us of his son Ian, and me talking back about my daughter Jocelyn. The coincidence was unbelievable. When I later told Tony about this, he was also amazed, but somewhat unsettled that his other living son's name was also on it. He said that was probably to let me know that it was HIS Ian. Yes, the grave had been there, my mother would later confirm. But how could we not have seen it. There was a reason we didn't. For some reason, at the time we were not suppose to see it. It was an amazing gift to get on our anniversary.

We visit her as much as we can. Anytime the question is asked, "what do you want to do today?" I immediately say, "I want to go to see my baby." Sometimes it works and sometimes it doesn't. I do go as much as I can. The best memory I have, after the anniversary even, was the special memorial mass they had at the cemetery for pregnancy and infant loss. The mass was held in the mausoleum where her funeral had been. The mass started and the priest read beautiful passages from the bible, all about babies. It was very comforting.

There were many people there, all in my shoes. That also put me at ease. Everyone there, whether they lost their children this year, last year, or fifteen years ago was there, hearts still breaking for the child they barely got to know. Tears still streaming down their cheeks.

That's when I realized the most that this will always be a huge part of my life. This will not be something I will get over in a week or a month, or even years and years from now. No other children we have will replace her, or even take away the pain of losing her. It was very nice, because although parents were still grieving over their own babies, they still came over to me and asked questions about my Jocelyn…all exclaiming what a beautiful name she had. And she did, I agree. After the mass was over, the priest blessed the porcelain angels and bears they had lined up on a table in the back. We each grabbed a few (some for home and some for their graves), and went outside.

From there, everyone lit a candle and walked from the chapel, across the yard to Baby Land, all in a hurry to get to our own babies. I got to Joc's grave, and my father in law, mother and law, sister in law, and myself all placed our candles on the four corners of the grave. We stood looking at the glow that seemed ever so gorgeous since nighttime had fallen. We stood back, and admired the new "Baby Land."

The place was lit up. It was a grand night. The candles illuminated the angels that we had all so lovingly placed on the graves of our own little angels. So wonderful to have so many people there. People who loved their babies just as much as I did. Some even wore tee shirts that said "In Memory of...." on the back. The lanterns that have become a custom to hang in Baby Land at your child's grave began turning on, the darker it got, and we all just stood around, enjoying the glow of this magical place. A place we all trusted to leave our angels at. Parents loving their children with everything they had, and now, I was one of them. And I belonged—yes, I belonged. Standing there with my pride and joy admiring the lights of "Baby Land" I could only imagine her view of the lights. Up there in the clouds with all her friends, looking down on Baby Land. It must have been magnificent!

Our baby girl, Jocelyn Nichole will always have a place in our hearts. We lost her, but are still a family. We will always know where to find her when we need to talk, or just need to know. She's up there in the clouds, and many times I look up and just say, "hey baby, mamma loves you". We have so many people to thank for bringing us through this experience. An experience that has taught us numerous lessons. Mostly, we want to thank God. To thank Him for the eight months of beautiful memories, spent with our daughter, for the chance to give birth to her, to see her, to hold her, and then to be able to place our perfect, sinless daughter in to His hands, where we know she will always be safe, and where she will never have to be scared, hungry, cold, or alone. Where she will be happy, where she can dance, dance in the clouds of Heaven. So to my daughter, I write these final words to you. You are our angel now, and we are forever grateful that you came into our lives. We wouldn't of traded you for a dozen healthy babies for anything in this world... We love you so, so much, and are so very proud of you. We look to the heavens and know you are there dancing and twirling around in your pretty white dress. Dancing around like little girls do. You will forever live in our hearts. We love our little angel, and hope you keep on dancing. Dance my little angel, and be at peace.

There are many reasons why I wrote this. First and most importantly, so that the few memories I have, her whole lifetime's worth, will always be remembered. So that when the memories begin fading away or becoming blurry, I will always have something to look back on. Also, it has helped me to release all that I was feeling. To get it off my chest and onto paper was the best therapy I could have done.

When I first began writing, just two weeks after losing her, I thought to myself, "what am I doing? You'll never make it through something like this without balling your eyes out every sentence." Yes, there were moments where I'd become choked up, or my eyes would tear up, but for the most part, I sailed through, just desperate to get all I could down.

Another reason for this book is due to the excellent advice from my friend Tony writing me very in depth letters about the similar experience he went through two years prior, and how he dealt with it. This helped me deal with the initial shock of it all.

Having someone right away who understood exactly what I was going through was a tremendous support. It was a blessing that I truly hope everyone could have while going through a tragedy. Immediate support from family is wonderful, but to have a connection already formed made a huge impact on how I was to further cope. I was taken aback and literally amazed how similar our situations were. The advice he gave me kept me strong, and so if I can pass on just a little of that advice, I might be able to help someone else who is going through this.

By reading or hearing about other people who have gone through what you are going through helps you to understand that you are not the only one. It seems like it, especially if it catches you blindsided, but in fact 1 in every 115 babies born are still. That is approximately 25,000 stillbirths in the United States each year.

I feel that if this book can help just one person cope with even a piece of their trial then I have given back what was given so nobly to me. Everyone deals with stillbirth differently. No experience is the same, and no one person will feel exactly as another, however, there are ways of coping that anyone can try. I will explain some of the ways I dealt with my own loss, and the grieving process that I went through.

What I have learned through this process is that first and foremost, no one understands exactly what you're going

ANDREA WAUN

through unless they've been through it themselves You will hear people talk, but will not understand the words that are coming from their mouths. The best thing to do in this situation is try and retain whatever you can, because it will hit you later. Words that people said right in the middle of your heartache will come back to you later, and it will strengthen you. You will be able to understand that mostly they were just trying to be supportive, but there will be things said that can actually give you strength later in the process.

The next thing I did was I made sure to give myself time to grieve. There is a process we all must go through. I would later find out through my own process that not going through each step can affect you, you're family, or your marriage. The steps of grieving will come as they please and give no warning when they will change.

One day you feel like its all okay, which is usually denial, and the next you are balling your eyes out. Often when I would wake up in the morning I would be in a fog. The depression and anxiety were a daily factor in my life and I had to learn how to take each step one at a time. I had to learn that I had little control over how I would feel from one moment to another. Sometimes it goes minute by minute and you feel like you can't possibly handle the overwhelming sense of so many emotions flooding you at once. However, the good news is that it gets better with time. If you follow your emotions and give yourself plenty of time to grieve, it eventually begins to clear up and things begin to once again slow down.

As you take time to go through the grieving process, also make sure to take care of yourself. In the midst of the heartache, planning, and confusion, it is easy to stop taking

54

care of yourself physically. Eating well and getting as much rest as you can will help your body physically, and in turn help you to stay more emotionally focused. The other side of this is if you find yourself doing nothing but sleeping through the day, unable to find energy to rise, then you can be safe in the assumption that depression has found you.

If you feel that you just can't make yourself eat or sleep, put someone you care about in charge of your eating and sleeping schedules. It is hard to do, but will help your body to heal quicker. The most sudden of changes that comes with any tragedy is the disruption of your routine. We all have one, simple or complex. We are all creatures of habit by nature and depression will typically steer us away from those little things that we did—accidentally on purpose'.

If you simply can't stomach food, or can't sleep at night, you may want to consult your doctor. Eating disorders are often times the result of stress, both in over or under eating. Part of it for me was that I was instinctually wanting to take care of my daughter, feeling that was my job now that I couldn't do and therefore stopped taking care of myself. I would find myself skipping meals without thought or staring into the cabinets and freezer with for what seemed like an hour unable to make that simple decision as to what to eat.

Talk to people or even just one other person who's been through this. You will see from them that life does go on, no matter how blinded you are to that concept at the time. If you are dealing with this process alone, get help through books, internet sites, or support groups. Talking to other people about what has happened to you when you don't even understand it all yourself is a very hard thing to do. Listening to other people's stories is also hard, but both will let you know that you are not alone in this. There are ways of getting past the darkness and seeing the light again.

Let others help you. You want to push them all away a lot of the time, but let them help. Listen to what they say. A lot of it is garbage, I admit, like all the "I understands," and "It'll be okays". Those will just infuriate you, because unless they've been through it, they don't understand, and when you're right in the middle of feeling the worst you've ever felt in your life, at that time, in your mind, it won't get better. People will say things that make you mad, and you should get mad. People will say things that make you want to cry—CRY.

One of the hardest parts of the process for me was to realize that you are not the same person as you were before. It's a very confusing feeling because you are the same person on the outside, but so much has changed on the inside that nothing feels right. You will feel as though you're going crazy, and that is normal. You will try like hell to be who you were before, or like we would say "we just want everything to get back to normal."

What is also hard is to recall the little things that gave you pleasure, happiness, or fulfillment. It's hard to find a sense of accomplishment when there is nothing you want to accomplish. But force yourself into your old hobbies. If you knit, start a sweater. If you play an instrument, compose your pain into a symphony even if only for yourself. Your sense of self is as complex as all the things that make you feel happy as well as what makes you sad, lonely, and inspired. Missing the happiness of yourself, is like losing yourself. Forcing yourself back into the things that brought you joy, even if only for a few moments of joy, sheds a bit of light into your world to show you the darkness isn't everlasting.

I would often try to trick my mind into thinking it was all just a really bad nightmare. It didn't seem real, and I didn't seem real. Your life changes drastically within seconds, and that was very hard for me to cope with. For the most part, life will get pretty close to what it was before, however, you have lost a very important piece of who you were, and that is the child that lived within you. Missing that piece changes who you are as any death or trauma will. Try to accept these changes as part of the new you.

You will never be exactly who you were. The reason for this is that a huge piece of your life has been taken literally from you, and you can't hide from that and pretend it never happened. For some of you, you probably felt your baby move, as I did, just days before you held her in your arms. It will be hard, I won't lie, but the cloudy skies, heavy heart, and inability to focus will go away. There really is no way to get through the whole process easily.

After time, though you get use to you're new identity of being a mother without a child. It's like (for the mothers anyway) every morning when you wake up, and through most of every day, you will try to validate to yourself that you are a mother. You were pregnant, gave birth, held your baby, but when you come home, where is that baby? You feel empty, and long for it all to be just a really bad dream.

Try to fight as few battles as you can. If you are having anxiety and you more than likely will, and your Dr has prescribed medicine, take it. If there is a support group near you, try it out, even once. If there is a list of to do's on your fridge or bills that need to be paid, let someone help you with that. Don't try to tackle everything on your own. You will most likely become frustrated and spiral backwards. Always try to move forward by doing whatever you can to make this tough experience as easy as you can.

Try to find a positive reasoning for negative thoughts. Thoughts will whirl through your head, and I'll tell you now, they are not pretty. Ugly thoughts of bad things happening to everyone else you love. Like seeing your baby's face spinning around and around you. I would see my child's face anytime I opened my eyes. I was glad of it in a way, but it got to the point where I felt like I was going crazy. I kept telling her how much I loved her and how much I missed her every time I saw her face, and eventually, that went away too. I choose to see her when I want now and that works better for me. Think the thoughts that run through your mind. Don't try to block them.

I also worried constantly about losing my husband. I guess after such a sudden loss, you are just insecure about what could happen next. The fear gripped me and wouldn't let go. Anytime he's leave for work, I'd wonder if he was coming back. I'd worry myself sick about whether he'd been in a car accident if he was even a few minutes late. I called his work constantly to make sure he was okay. I went along with these thoughts, and said to myself, any time we're together, we must love each other with everything we have. We must make the best of every single minute we're given together. We did just that. Although we were coping in different ways, Jocelyn was with us, and pulled us closer in those moments. She made our marriage strong during those first crucial months, and we hung to each other with faith and hope.

A huge part of this that I really haven't touched on, as this is my personal experience, is the experience of your partner. You can not discount the feelings, emotions, struggle, and pain that he will be going through and may hide from you to shelter you from any more pain than you already have to face. Tony helped me to understand that and thus helped me to nurture my marriage through it all.

My husband had lost a child as well and never knew the joys of the kicking, hiccups, and rolls she took inside me. But he knew the joy of waiting and anticipating a new chapter of our lives. He knew that he had already found love to one he had never met that was strong enough to love for the rest of his life and had it taken away. It is easy to assume your pain is simply worse than his, but they are not identical experiences and there for can not be measured as to who is suffering more.

What we are all searching for is some level of peace. Find what it was in life that made you truly at peace. For me it was Christian music. I listened to a catholic hymn from our church that has a line in it that always comforted me. "be not afraid— I go before you always, come follow Me, and I will give you strength." I listened to this daily, until one day, I just didn't have that fear anymore. I crocheted blankets as I always had which was a comfort to me, and of course, began writing which I have always enjoyed. You must allow yourself to have some joy in your life, a moment of peace and sanity in a world that seems to have gone mad. To me, it was a release I needed and a way to get away without actually running away.

Each night my sleep was interrupted, which made it very hard to function. Nightmares consumed my sleep every night since her passing, and are only now, starting to get better. I am on a sleep medication that will help with this, but how terrible it has been to not only have to deal with the pain and memories of losing your child while you're awake, but also while you're asleep. It just kept replaying and replaying itself. I would see my daughter's lifeless form every single night, and when I woke in the morning would find myself buried beneath a thick cloud of depression. It plagued me. I chose to get on a sleep medication to help me to get past these horrid images. After a few months, they began to subside.

Another bit of advice is to face everything. Face it head on as soon as it hits you. If you bury anything, it will eventually weigh you down, and you will more than likely have more problems in the future. Also, don't be afraid to try new tactics of coping. The things I say helped me, but may not help you. See if new ideas work. If they do, add them to your routine. If they don't, discard of them. Try not to feel too sorry for yourself. Always remind yourself that God did this for a reason. There's a reason for everything.

If you need to feel sorry for yourself once in a while, do it. Anyone who's been through this knows you have that right. Just don't let it weigh you down. The best thing to do and I recommend this highly—stay busy. My parents had me out doing lawn work, helping with their garage sale, things of that nature. Do things to where you are around people, but make sure you are able to get away whenever you want or need to. That is important. Give yourself plenty of time to sleep. Your body and mind have been taken to their limit, and you don't even realize it at first. When it hits you, that's when you're done and struggle to recover even harder. You can take no more. That's what happened to me.

For the first few days, I wouldn't rest. I knew my baby had not been properly laid to rest, so I wouldn't rest either. Even if I had wanted to, I couldn't. After her funeral was over, I was completely wiped out. My body ached, and I just felt completely done. For weeks after, you will try different routines. Some will work and some will not. Some will work one day, but not another. It will be extremely confusing, and mind altering, but it will become clear, and your life will slowly begin to take shape again. Try not to rush anything. There is no time limit to feel better.

As I myself found out quickly through Tony, who after two years can still sit down and painstakingly write the story of his son's life. And lastly, try to get your story out, one way or another. You don't have to sit and write a novel, but get your best and most wonderful memories into some sort of organized form. Make a memory box, tell a friend, have a special song that you dedicate to the memory of your child, or, like me, you can get on your computer and just type. The words seem to just come.

Whatever your way is, do something that helps you to release it from the inside of yourself and put it out for the world to see. Remember, your child will always have a place in your heart, nothing can change that, so don't be afraid to let stuff go. This will become your own personal experience, and in the end you will look back and be able to list the things you got from this: Some positive, others not. For me, I look upon this as a positive experience. I am overly grateful to the Lord for just letting me have those few moments with her; for being able to see what she looks like and to hold her. It hurt then, but now, I am at peace knowing that my child is dancing in the clouds.

I will honestly say that if I could have had another child at the same time, a healthy child, but it would not be my Joc, I wouldn't take it, because there is no promise for a long life for anyone, and the few moments I had with my daughter meant everything and will carry me through the rest of my life. I wouldn't of traded that beautiful baby girl for anything in this world.

To me I can now put another piece into my puzzle in realizing that life truly is just that—a puzzle. The corners are basically given to you through who you were made to be by personality, traits, genes, etc. Many pieces are handed to you throughout your childhood by the way you were raised and the morals and values you were taught. The rest of the time, you work to fill in the rest. Learning, you might want to call it. You fill in one piece at a time. Sometimes you rush and try to fill in too many and mistakes happen. Other times you get bored with the puzzle, also known as laziness, and just sit around hoping someone puts some of your pieces in for you.

Other times you work hard and feel a sense of accomplishment for a huge portion of your puzzle getting complete. Then there are those times where someone or something comes along and rips apart your puzzle. These are those moments of pain, rejection, betrayal, that seem to take you backwards in life. Then there are those moments when you feel like just giving up on the puzzle, God puts in a few pieces for you. These are blessings. We work so hard to fill in the pieces of our lives, thinking to ourselves that maybe tomorrow it will be done.

I have realized through these experiences of mine that the puzzle will only be as complete as you make it until you die.

You can only hope that your puzzle is as complete as you want it to be. I also believe that God has some of the pieces that he doesn't want you to have. We want things right now. Good things to happen. A pay raise, a loving partner to share life with, to win the lottery, a new house….and very often these things come to us…in time. The saying "God has a plan for us" says a lot when He is in control of our lives. He holds the pieces we are sometimes desperately looking for. Maybe we'll get them in this world, and maybe we'll have to wait for the next. Either way, I have begun to fill up my puzzle with the pieces I know I have. Love, kindness, giving, laughter, a good attitude, etc are all examples I use on a daily basis to try to piece together my puzzle.

So many times I have done this, and it seems that something always happens that tears my hard work apart, but I have learned that no one and nothing can completely wipe out your whole puzzle. I believe the puzzle will be complete when we get to Heaven and all our answers are sitting before us in a beautiful picture—our puzzle—our life.

Nearly two years since losing Jocelyn, sadly, Alex and I lost two others due to miscarriage. We had dealt with losing our daughter in the best way we both knew how, but both knew we were living and coping with it in completely different ways. We held on to each other as best we could, but with one person trying to fight to move slowly through the steps of grieving and the other wanting simply to let it all go and bury it, it became hard to stay on the same page of the book. A year after losing Jocelyn, and yet another baby, we both could see that we were beginning to spiral out of control. Our marriage became strained and I fought to try and save it. It was simply too late.

Alex had met someone else, unknownst to me, and was living the double life. Something, despite the betrayal I felt, I would later make me realize that this was the only way he could escape the pain and grief he had so long buried. Such a young couple with so much loss in our wakes. What can be done? I saw things as a positive. Everything happens for a reason, the glass is half full. He on the other hand saw his world being torn apart anytime the sun began to shine. Although the affair itself nearly tore my spirits apart, I wanted to make the marriage work. I wouldn't give up on my dreams. Unfortunately, the details of the affair would not let that happen. Alex had found love, and chose to leave the marriage. We were divorced shortly after. I would later find out the statistics of young couples and the proximation of how much work is involved when losing multiple children. After Alex made the choice to leave the marriage, I found myself alone, and once again pregnant. Not knowing that I was pregnant, I did not take care of myself, and lost that baby as well. It goes to show that somewhere amidst all of our plans and dreams of what we want to happen in our lives, sometimes, there is a purpose we don't really see until it is handed to us in bomb form. A blast that knocks you backwards and makes you really and truly re evaluate your life. Amidst going through the steps of grieving again through losing my husband I did just that. I talked to God and told him that I was trying to be in control of my life, whereas I knew now that a plan had already been set. It has been nearly three years since the death of my first child until now, and miraculously, I am feeling the best I've felt in my life. Despite the wrongs Alex has done, when I talk to him now, I see the man I fell in love with ten years ago. He is happy and although I yearned to be the one to make him happy, it wasn't in God's plan. I have forgiven him, because I know that tragedies of this nature can make a person do things they never thought they would. Alex to me will always have a wonderful heart, and continue to care for others as he always has, and I believe that he has become a better person throughout this experience. For me on the other hand, I too have found happiness in my own life. I am independent, and have found support, love and guidance through my friends, family, and of course my best friend, Tony. Although Alex and I live separate lives now, we know we will always be a family, and what bonds us together is our beautiful children. I truly believe that unknownst to each of us, we were slowly tearing eachother apart trying to deal with so much loss. I believe also that Jocelyn's purpose was fulfilled in making us each better people, and I thank her for showing us what we could not see. That God has our lives in his hands, and we are not in charge of our destinies. The paths we must follow now will lie in the hands of our Lord and with the guidance of four little angels in heaven, one named Jocelyn Nichole. So, with that said, I end the story of our family, not saddened, but uplifted, knowing that for just a brief point in my long life, I had a family, and that although the past cannot be changed, it is a chapter of my life that I will never ever forget. A family divided for the sake of making two people better at who they are.

My Thanks Go Out To

With the utmost gratitude, I extend my thanks to all who have supported me through this whole entire process.

First and foremost, to my family who stood by my side throughout the whole process. Through the confusion, the tears, the anger, and back again. Who gave me direction when at times I felt lost and out of control. You truly are the wind beneath my wings, and I couldn't of done it without your love and support.

Secondly, to Tony, who despite the overwhelming ordeals that he too has endured, stood strongly by my side, never budging once despite the rocky steps. I took him along to try to get myself out of my own mess. He followed me throughout, sometimes leading the way, sometimes following, but mostly right by my side where I needed him.

Thirdly, I want to thank the community of Holy Trinity Catholic Church who have had me in their prayers since the loss of my first child. Who have been the foundation I could fall upon when I felt myself spiraling downwards. Your prayers and kindness throughout the years have made me who I am. A faith filled individual, guided by the graces of God.

Fourthly, to Alex, who gave me the dream of holding my baby in my arms. Despite the loss of our marriage, we together went through these ordeals, living on faith. We didn't make it as a couple, but we fought a great battle. One that dealt us some pretty ugly cards. I know we will always be a family, and for those few precious moments with my daughter, with him standing by my side, I thank him.

And most importantly, to God, who knows me better than I know myself. Who holds my dear babies in the palm of his hands, and continues to watch over me, despite how stubborn I might be. I thank Him for the opportunity to be a family and to show us the way throughout this life. It is not always what you expect, but He will get you to where you need to be with a little faith in His plans for you.

Lightning Source UK Ltd.
Milton Keynes UK
UKOW051825200911

178989UK00001B/346/P